INVENTORS & INVENTIONS

SATELLITES

INVENTORS & INVENTIONS

SATELLITES

MARY VIRGINIA FOX

BENCHMARK BOOKS

MARSHALL CAVENDISH

NEW YORK

Benchmark Books
Marshall Cavendish Corporation
99 White Plains Road
Tarrytown, New York 10591-9001

Series created by The Creative Publishing Company

Library of Congress Cataloging-in-Publication Data

Fox, Mary Virginia.
   Satellites / Mary Virginia Fox.
      p.   cm. -- (Inventors & inventions)
   Includes index.
   Summary: Describes the development and deployment of man-made satellites and surveys their many varied uses--past, present, and future.
   ISBN 0-7614-0049-4 (lib. bdg.)
   1. Artificial satellites--Juvenile literature.   [1. Artificial satellites.]   I. Title.   II. Series.
TL796.F69   1996
629.43--dc20   95-41574
                                                         CIP
                                                         AC

Printed in Hong Kong

Acknowledgments

Technical Consultant: Teodoro C. Robles, Ph.D.
Illustration on page 16 by Julian Baker

The publishers would like to thank the following for their permission to reproduce photographs:
NASA, (frontispiece, 13, 21, 32, 33, 36, 47, 49, 53); Novosti, (9, 12); Science & Society Picture Library, (25); Science Photo Library Ltd., (John Frassanito cover, NASA 7, Novosti 9, 12, NASA 14, 15, David Parker, ESA 17, NASA 19, 20, Tony Buxton 23, NASA 27, David Ducros/Jerrican 28, Julian Baum 30, NOAA 31, NASA GSFC 35, BP/NRSC 38, Earth Satellite Corporation 39, 40, NASA 42, 43, Peter Menzel 45, Space Telescope Science Institute/NASA 48, NASA 52, 54, 56, 57, 58, 59); UPI/Bettmann, (26, 44, 51).

(Cover) The space shuttle Atlantis *docks with the Russian space station* Mir.

(Frontispiece) Technicians at the Kennedy Space Center encapsulate satellites to be sent into orbit aboard a Delta rocket.

Contents

—— Chapter 1 ——
Watchful Eyes

On June 6, 1986, Dr. E. Jeff Justin and his wife, Sally, were flying their twin-engine plane over Greenland's ice cap when both engines failed. There was nothing they could do but land in an uninhabited area on a rough plateau of ice 9,300 feet (2,800 meters) above sea level.

A storm was moving in fast. Only one very special bit of equipment saved their lives — a small emergency locator transmitter, no larger than a portable phone.

Their distress signal was broadcast to the satellite search and rescue system, which automatically redirected the message to a receiving station on the ground. An exact bearing of their location was recorded, and within two hours, a Danish helicopter picked them up.

Without such a prompt reply, they would have perished. Weather would have blocked any hope of recovery for at least a week, and there would have been no chance of their being able to remain alive in such a brutal environment.

The concept for a satellite-aided search and rescue project (SARSAT) began almost as soon as the United States placed its first satellite in orbit. Later, the Soviet Union agreed to equip their COSMOS satellites with the same equipment, so that now the entire surface of the Earth is monitored.

Ships at sea and expeditions into remote parts of our planet now have a way of telling exactly where they are and sending for help if needed. The SARSAT program has been instrumental not only in saving hundreds of lives but also in saving millions of dollars in search efforts.

Objects on High

Far above our planet, sometimes visible but most often not, metal machines peer down on us. Others train their gaze out to the stars and to the galaxies beyond our own. Some allow scientists to explore Earth's surface, while others help telephone, television, and radio signals circle the globe, enabling people to communicate across oceans and mountains. Information and statistics on weather, geology, emissions from the Sun and from stars are all beamed to ground-based receiving stations where, slowly, we are forming an ever-clearer picture of our planet and our universe.

An artist's impression of Wind *and* Polar, *two satellites launched during the 1990s to study the interactions between Earth and the Sun.* Wind, *left, orbits at high altitude, studying solar wind while* Polar, *placed in an orbit much closer to Earth, investigates the Sun's effect on our atmosphere.*

While the term satellite can also mean a natural body circling a planet or other object in space, in this book we will be discussing human-made objects, machines, and space vehicles in orbit. Even humans in space, if they're going around the planet, can be considered satellites. Some satellites are currently helping us understand the birth of our universe, but their own beginnings are recent, indeed.

First in Space

A rocket towering 92 feet (28 meters) above the isolated, treeless land stood ready for launch. Few Soviets knew it existed, and even fewer knew what it would be carrying into outer space. The date was October 4, 1957; the place, Tyuratum, USSR.

On the other side of the world, the Soviet embassy in Washington, D.C., was entertaining a group of scientists. 1957 was International Geophysical Year, when sixty-six countries were participating in complex projects, from ocean currents to cosmic ray detection. The United States proposed sending probes deep into space to analyze the content of Earth's atmosphere in the upper reaches beyond the cloud cover. If a rocket were to be sent into outer space, it was important to have radio equipment tuned to a proper frequency to monitor the data around the world. The discussion continued even as the group was being served refreshments.

Dr. Lloyd Berkner, an American guest, was called to the phone. A newspaper reporter gave him startling news — a radio signal had been heard coming from a mysterious satellite that was even then circling Earth. Could Berkner give the public any more information about the event?

It was clear to Berkner that the only other country with rockets powerful enough to put a satellite in space was the Soviet Union. They had accomplished what others were still dreaming of doing. It should be a moment of celebration, even if a disappointment to the American delegation that had hoped to be the

---

AMAZING FACTS

Before anyone had placed an artificial satellite in orbit, U.S. Army engineers beamed a radio signal to the surface of the Moon, Earth's natural satellite. In turn, the signal bounced back to Earth, making it the first attempt at space communication.

first in space. Berkner quickly brought the group of scientists to attention.

He proposed a toast. "I wish to compliment our Soviet colleagues on their achievement."

Bombarded by questions, Soviet scientist Sergei Blagonravov revealed that the satellite, named *Sputnik*, meaning "traveling companion" in Russian, was but a test to see if the launching system worked. He drew a picture of a sphere, to which were attached four antennae that had been extended after the shiny ball reached its final orbit. He told his fellow scientists that the sphere was filled with nitrogen gas, which acted as an air conditioning system. The radio signals were simply meant to transmit the temperature of the satellite as it moved from scorching sunlight to frigid blackness on the night side of the orbit. If a tiny meteorite should pierce the satellite skin, the message would be relayed to Earth.

The Space Race

One reason the United States was so far behind the Soviets was that American scientists had developed a deadly, efficient, lightweight nuclear bomb that did not take such a powerful rocket to launch. The Soviets had to develop stronger firepower to propel the much larger warheads in their bomb arsenal. These rockets proved strong enough to send an object beyond Earth's atmosphere. The United States now found itself racing to catch up with Soviet rocket design.

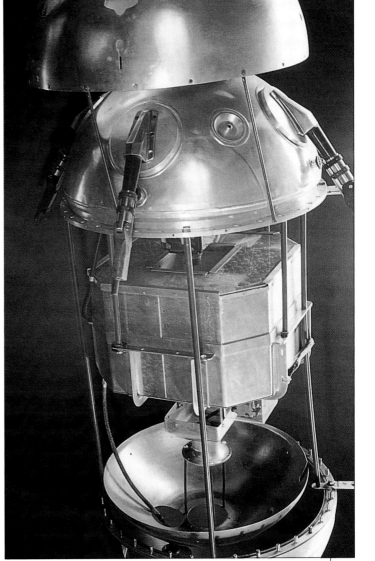

Sputnik 1, *the world's first artificial satellite, transmitted signals back to Earth for twenty-one days. The parts shown here formed a sphere twenty-three inches (fifty-eight centimeters) in diameter.*

Sergei Korolev (1906–1966)

Even after the launch of their first satellite, the Soviets continued to be very secretive about their space program. Only after the death in 1966 of Sergei Korolev did they reveal any details about the life of the one man who was largely responsible for the success of *Sputnik*.

Korolev was born in 1906 in the Ukraine, in the southwestern part of the former USSR. (It's now an independent country.) He saw his first airplane when Sergei Utochkin, a famous Soviet flyer, demonstrated his flying skill on the outskirts of Nezhin, where Korolev and his family lived. The dashing pilot made such an impression on the young man that from that moment on, Korolev decided he would study all he could about aeronautics.

It was not easy to find such training. Instead, he entered a technical school for construction workers and learned the trade of a roofer, though he refused to give up his earlier ambition. He joined a glider club and designed his own engineless craft. His application for admission to the Air Force Academy was turned down because

Sergei Korolev, second from right, with fellow Soviet scientists and engineers on a picnic in 1934. They were all members of a group he had helped set up in 1932 to study jet propulsion.

there were too many other young men who wanted to become flyers at the time.

Instead, Korolev went to Moscow and entered the country's best engineering school. He was successful in building the first glider able to execute three loops in flight. He also tried designing light airplanes and finally obtained a pilot's license in 1930.

He was fascinated by articles written by a fellow Russian, Konstantin E. Tsiolkovsky, who felt that rocket power would be the future of high-altitude flying. Korolev joined an organization of young scientists who were working on designs for liquid-fueled rockets. The group's headquarters was in the basement of an apartment building near the center of Moscow. Tests were secretly conducted outside the city.

Sergei Korolev, right, with Yuri Gagarin, the first man in space.

During World War II, Korolev designed rockets that were used to improve the performance of fighter planes. By 1947, he had been named chief of the USSR's Experimental Design Bureau, designing rockets for both peaceful and military purposes. Sergei Korolev's identity was not revealed to the public because the Soviets said they were afraid he might be kidnapped by Western countries to learn the secrets of Soviet technology.

However, at his death, the official obituary credited him with being the man who made possible the launching of the world's first satellite. It was Korolev who had drawn the final specifications for the satellite and rocket, after months of calculating the relation between thrust and weight of an object entering orbit. His ashes were buried in a niche in the Kremlin Wall, an area reserved for heroes of the USSR.

On January 2, 1959, the Soviet spacecraft *Luna 1* was the first to escape Earth's gravity. It missed the Moon and went into orbit around the Sun, between the orbits of Earth and Mars.

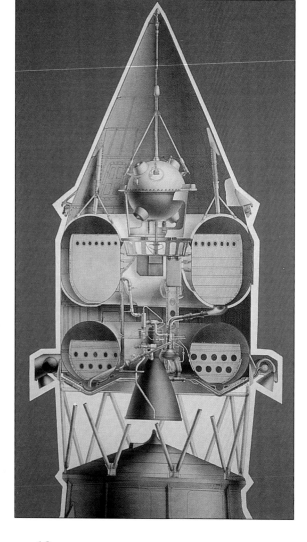

A diagram of the Soviet Luna 1 *spacecraft.*

The biggest blow to American pride was to learn that *Sputnik* weighed 184 pounds (83 kilograms), much larger than the satellite the United States was planning to put into space. What the Soviets were not willing to share at this time was the size and design of the rocket that had launched *Sputnik*. This frightened American scientists. With this much power, the Soviet Union could easily put an atomic bomb into orbit that could be aimed at the United States.

The launch of the first *Sputnik* came as a tremendous shock to the Western world, which had up to then tended to underestimate Soviet technical abilities. To try to restore confidence in their own accomplishments, the schedule for an American satellite launch was moved ahead.

American Failures

On December 6, 1957, just two months after the launch of *Sputnik 1*, the Vanguard rocket stood on its launch site at Cape Canaveral, Florida. Cameras were ready. Excitement mounted, but two seconds after ignition, the rocket blew itself to pieces in a huge fireball.

To make matters worse for the United States, a second attempt by a Vanguard rocket also ended in failure, while the Soviets had been able to launch another satellite, this time with the tremendous weight of 1,140 pounds (513 kilograms), carrying a living passenger.

A dog named Laika traveled in an airtight container supplied with food and water in the form of gelatin. Fresh air of a comfortable temperature and humidity was provided. Laika remained alive in her space capsule for a week, until electric power failed and the satellite became silent.

Success at Last

By this time, the National Aeronautical and Space Administration (NASA) had decided to replace the Vanguard rocket with a more reliable, modified Redstone missile, which had been designed by Wernher von Braun (a rocket scientist from Germany) to carry warheads. On January 31, 1958, *Explorer 1* went into orbit. It was 80 inches (203 centimeters) long, six inches (15 centimeters) in diameter and weighed slightly more than thirty pounds (13.5 kilograms). It carried eighteen pounds (eight kilograms) of advanced scientific instruments. As with the Soviet *Sputnik 1* and *2*, *Explorer 1* was put into elliptical orbit, climbing as high as 1,573 miles (2533 kilometers) and coming as close to Earth as 224 miles (361 kilometers).

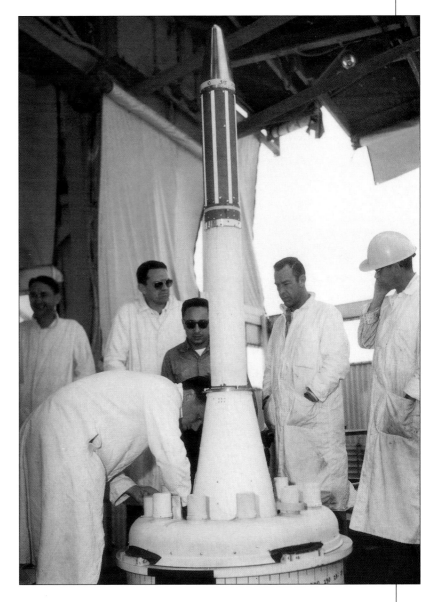

Its most important discovery was the presence of highly charged radioactive particles trapped by Earth's magnetic field. This unexpected phenomenon was called the *Van Allen Radiation Belt*, in honor of the scientist directing the mission. At first, it was thought that the radiation would hinder any further exploration of space. This theory proved false when instruments returned to Earth unharmed. Scientists were already designing more sophisticated equipment to monitor what other surprises outer space would bring.

Technicians prepare Explorer 1 *for launch at Cape Canaveral, Florida. The satellite was built under the direction of James Van Allen of the Jet Propulsion Laboratory at the California Institute of Technology.*

The United States followed this success with rockets that took chimpanzees, Able, Baker, and Ham, into space. The chimps had been trained to push certain levers to deliver their food, thus proving that maneuvers requiring thought were possible even while the chimps were enduring zero gravity and the pressure of both takeoff and landings.

Chimpanzee Ham alive and well after his flight on January 31, 1961. Although his body was subjected to seventeen times the force of gravity on launch, six minutes of weightlessness, and a splashdown in the Atlantic Ocean, Ham lived for another twenty-two years. Experiments like this convinced scientists that humans, too, could survive in space.

Still, the Soviets outdid the United States in sending larger and larger satellites; *Sputnik 3* carried 2,129 pounds (958 kilograms) of instruments, while Americans had sent no more than 65 pounds (29 kilograms) into space.

The USSR's greatest achievement was announced on April 12, 1961, when Yuri Gagarin became the first human to orbit Earth and safely parachuted down near the Volga River 25,000 miles (40,000 kilometers) and 108 minutes after liftoff.

Next it would be the United States' turn to introduce astronauts; more powerful rockets and larger space capsules were being prepared for them. But in the meantime, the United States was developing ways to use unpiloted satellites to help study the heavens and send messages around the world.

Chapter 2
How Satellites Stay Up in Space

To put a satellite in orbit around Earth, a rocket must be traveling at a tremendous speed to escape the pull of Earth's gravity. Once it is in orbit, the satellite can keep going with very little power because gravity is no longer strong enough to bring it crashing back to Earth.

The rocket that launches a satellite is usually a multistage rocket. With the most powerful thrust, the first stage takes the satellite through the densest layer of the atmosphere. When the fuel of the first stage is used up, the rocket engine and the fuel tank drop away, and the next stage ignites and boosts the satellite even higher. As the rocket becomes lighter in weight, not as much power is needed to send it even farther in space.

An American Satellite Company (ASC) communication satellite is launched from the cargo bay of space shuttle Discovery *during a 1985 mission. Shuttles have a jointed arm that enables them to put a wide variety of satellites into orbit.*

Some of our satellites have been carried partway on their journey into space by one of our fleet of space shuttles. When satellites are released from the cargo bay of the shuttle, they may then be sent even farther into space by much smaller rockets that can be controlled from Earth. These built-in rockets that make minor adjustments in their orbit are called *thrusters*.

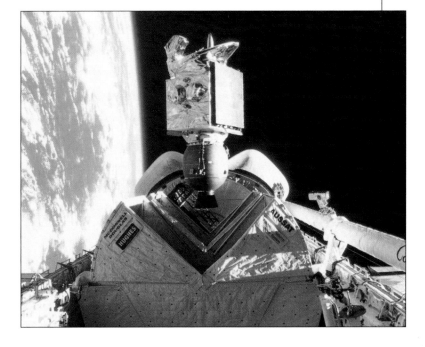

Satellites in Orbit

Imagine what happens when a small weight is tied to a string and swung around in a circle. If the string were to break, the weight would fly off in a straight line. The string acts like gravity, keeping the weight in orbit. If you lengthen the string and swing it in a circle, you will see that the weight takes a longer time to complete the circle. This is what happens when a satellite is put into a higher orbit; it takes longer to circle Earth the farther away it is.

The orbit of a satellite depends on what it is programmed to observe. Some satellites that orbit Earth are close enough to be seen by observers with binoculars. Others have been placed in orbit some 70,000 miles (112,000 kilometers) above Earth.

Satellites do not always travel in a perfect circle. They may follow an elliptical path where they can measure elements in

Satellites are designed to gather a wide range of information so their paths around and heights above Earth are not all the same. This illustration shows three common Earth orbits.

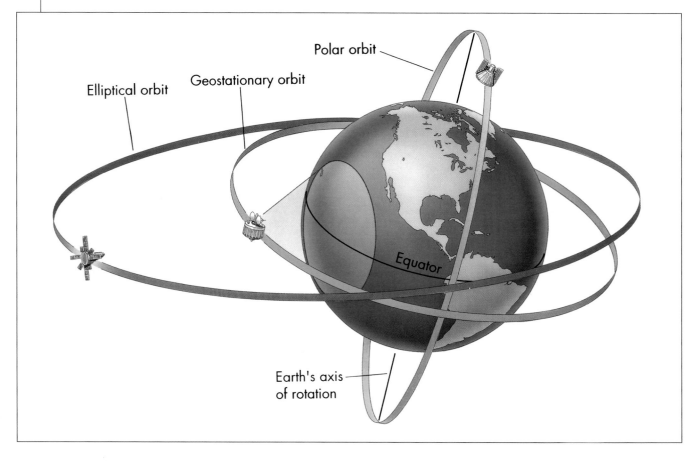

deep space and then head back toward Earth only to repeat their orbit.

A satellite that is positioned over one specific point on Earth's equator is said to be in *geostationary orbit*. This means it is "keeping up" with the rotation of Earth. Earth makes one full turn every twenty-four hours. A satellite can also be programmed to make a complete orbit in twenty-four hours, but it has to be at an elevation of 22,300 miles (35,900 kilometers) above Earth. Farther out in space, it takes longer to circle our planet. A lower orbit requires fewer hours.

Some satellites revolve roughly from north to south, passing over Earth's poles. A *sun-synchronized polar orbit* is coordinated with Earth's movement around the Sun in such a way that the satellite always crosses the equator at the same local time. One of our weather monitors always crosses the equator at 1:40 A.M. and 1:40 P.M. Eastern Standard Time.

Many satellites travel around Earth close to the equator. Launch sites near the equator are ideal for these satellites since they get a certain natural boost from the rotation of Earth itself as it spins faster at the equator.

Satellites far out into space may stay in orbit forever. Only if their speed decreases and Earth's gravity pulls them down into a relatively dense layer of atmosphere will they fall to Earth. A satellite slows down in the upper atmosphere due to the friction of air particles. It then rapidly compresses the air in front of it. The air becomes so hot that most satellites burn up in our atmosphere. That is the reason why both the Soviets and Americans had to develop foolproof insulation for their satellites before putting humans into space.

The first public exhibition of the European Space Agency's Ariane 4 rocket at Kourou, French Guiana, in 1988. Ariane rockets were designed for putting geostationary satellites in orbit, and this launch site is only about five degrees north of the equator, thus making the rocket's task easier. Ariane 4 is a versatile three-stage rocket with two to four strap-on boosters and a choice of caps to contain a wide range of satellites.

What Satellites Do

There are six main uses for artificial satellites: scientific research, communication, monitoring weather, studying Earth, immediately locating a ship or moving vehicle on Earth to help with navigation, and use by the military.

Satellites may be piloted, such as the space shuttles that orbit our Earth, or unpiloted, such as the tracking and data-relay satellites. They can be sent into space with the intention that they will not be recovered, or they may be designed to be recovered and repaired by space shuttle or space station crews. At this time, only the Russians have a working space station where crews of cosmonauts take turns in shifts to conduct research in space. However, the United States is planning one. It will be designed in sections to be put together up in space by astronauts and will be in operation by the turn of the century.

How Satellites Are Equipped

All artificial satellites have certain features in common. They include radar for altitude measurements and sensors, such as optical devices, to take pictures or produce numerical codes for what they are seeing. Radio transmitters and receivers send signals back and forth from space and sometimes position the antennae and sensors properly. Telemetry encoders, devices that measure distances and the angle of the satellite's path, keep track of the onboard equipment and relay this information in the form of a numerical code to Earth. Adjustments to all this equipment and to the satellite's path can be made by sending signals from Earth. Small thruster rockets can be fired to change the direction of a satellite's orbit.

Satellites are powered by solar cells, which store energy from the Sun; storage batteries are used for power during the periods when the satellite is blocked from the Sun by Earth. These batteries are, in turn, recharged by the solar cells. In special cases, nuclear power keeps the satellite in its desired orbit. Only a very minute quantity of material is used in this case, to keep the weight of a satellite at a minimum.

Of course, without computers to analyze the stream of information being sent from the hundreds of satellites now in space, we'd know very little about what is being observed.

Servicing in Space

Each year, we are discovering more ways to use these valuable devices circling overhead. And, as the need for more satellites continues to increase, NASA's budget is strained to cover these new projects.

Practical ways to service existing satellites are needed. Most of our current two hundred thousand satellites aren't wearing out; they just need to have fuel replaced in their small thrusters to keep them in the proper orbit.

In October 1984, one of the first trial runs to do this required the two astronauts aboard the space shuttle, Kathryn Sullivan and David Leestma, to "step outside" to dock a satellite in the payload bay. They then did routine repair work and refueled the satellite's thrusters.

In the future, astronauts, and in some cases, robots, will be able to keep our fleet of satellites in operation longer.

Astronaut James van Hoften helps repair the Solar Maximum Mission (SMM) satellite in the cargo bay of the space shuttle Challenger *in 1984. The satellite was retrieved from orbit, a jammed communications antenna was freed, and the satellite was redeployed.*

Kathryn Sullivan

Kathryn Sullivan became the first woman to walk in space, the first to complete an EVA, Extra-Vehicular Activity, as NASA calls it. This was something she had been looking forward to from the moment she joined the elite astronaut corps in 1978, the youngest at the time. It was one of her ambitions even before that because Sullivan had hoped to become an astronaut from the moment she heard men were going to the Moon. She thought her father, an aeronautical engineer, and her brother, a jet pilot, were more likely candidates, but kid sister made the grade.

When asked how she trained for her job, she admits, "I had no special program for staying fit, but I'm pretty athletic and basically healthy. I run, play racquet ball, enjoy competitive sailing, and generally stay in motion as much as possible."

Sullivan was born in New Jersey in 1952, but her family soon moved to Woodland Hills, California. Her career training started with an earth science degree from the University of California, Santa Cruz. She spent one year as an undergraduate exchange student at the University of Bergen in Norway. It meant learning a new language, but Sullivan is a very outgoing person. It is important to her to communicate with people. By the time she graduated from college, she had mastered six languages.

"I'd never say mastered," Sullivan corrects, "but I can get by without too much trouble."

She earned her doctorate in geophysics at Dalhouse University in Halifax, Nova Scotia. She has taken part in a number of oceanic expeditions studying the bottom of the sea floor — the exact opposite direction from where she now focuses her sight. However, being on board a ship working on experiments isn't all that

Kathryn Sullivan and David Leestma aboard space shuttle Challenger *in October 1984.*

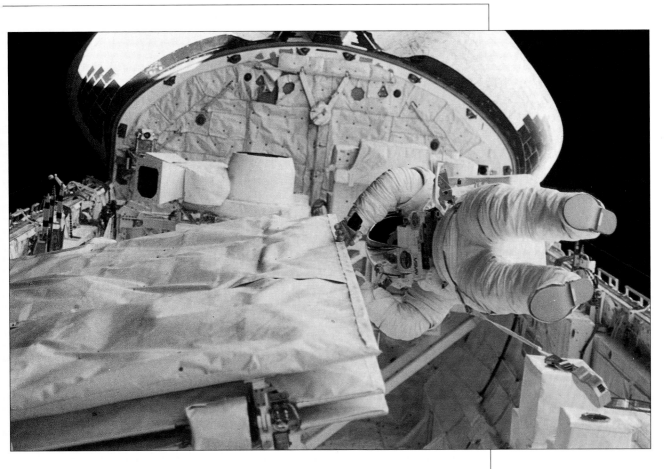

much different from her training on the space shuttle, working in close quarters with people in isolation. "Being five hundred miles out to sea is very similar to a space mission. You'd better have everything you need and plans for every contingency."

Sullivan has been on three shuttle missions, walking in space a second time when she and astronaut Bruce McCandless helped deploy a space telescope on April 25, 1990. A major antenna was snagged on a bowed electric cable. Their work helped save $1.5 billion worth of equipment.

Kathryn Sullivan's last trip in space was in 1992. She has recently retired, if one can call it that, to a teaching position. When astronauts are not in space, they are planning, studying, and equipping further projects that are leading the way for even more extensive exploration of space. As one of the first six women to be chosen to join the astronaut corps, she has led the way as a respected role model for others.

— Chapter 3 —
A Voice from Space

The first job given to satellites was to find out just what outer space was like. Would small meteors destroy satellites? What were the extremes of temperature? Would radiation from outer space put an end to the hope of human space exploration? Soon other, very practical and valuable uses were found for satellites. Perhaps the most important technical application was in the field of communication.

Echo, the first satellite to be used in this way, was launched in 1960. Nothing more than a huge plastic balloon coated with a very thin layer of aluminum, at takeoff it was folded into a small package. Only after reaching orbit was it inflated to its full 135-foot (41-meter) diameter. Radio transmitters on the ground beamed up signals that bounced back from its mirrorlike surface to receivers elsewhere on Earth.

This kind of *passive* satellite contains no radio transmitter or other energy system. It is very reliable because it has no electronic parts that can fail, but it requires powerful transmitters and sensitive receivers on the ground.

Communication satellites today carry equipment onboard to amplify the power of incoming signals before they are relayed back to a receiving station on Earth. Such a satellite requires solar cells to supply power to the amplifiers and fuel to the thrusters and controls that periodically adjust the satellite's position to keep antennae pointed properly to Earth.

The major Earth stations that communicate with these satellites typically use large, dish-shaped antennae at least one hundred feet (thirty meters) in diameter. The receivers are wrapped

AMAZING FACTS

Soviet engineers developed a mobile ground station, *Mars*, to reach a world audience of 2,000 to 2,500 million people watching the Moscow Olympics in 1980. Even though the main dish antenna was twenty-three feet (seven meters) in diameter, it was all transportable in three containers.

with refrigerated coils to reduce static, and radio transmitters with power output of several thousand watts are needed.

Linking America and Europe

Telstar 1 was launched on July 10, 1962, and was followed a year later by *Telstar 2*. Ground stations were located at Andover, Maine (USA), Goonhilly Downs (England), and Pleumeur-Bodou (France). The first broadcast, just fifteen hours after launch, showed a picture of the American flag flapping in the wind over the Andover station. Two weeks later, millions of Americans and Europeans watched and listened as a conversation was carried on between people on opposite sides of the Atlantic. Not only voices but pictures were relayed live via satellite. Headlines in newspapers proclaimed this the date of the birth of the "global village."

A communication Earth station in Hong Kong. The largest dishes communicate with the network of Intelsat satellites in geostationary orbit, while the smaller ones are linked to AsiaSat-1, a satellite providing communications across China, southeast Asia, and Pakistan.

23

Telstar 1 was followed by *Relay 1* and *Relay 2* — experimental vehicles, like *Telstar*, launched to discover what problems, if any, larger, more extensive arrays of equipment might have when put into space. It was discovered that radiation had a damaging effect on the solar cells that provided power. Although a great deal of research has helped lessen this problem, all communication satellites are sent aloft with more solar cells than are needed at first, with the expectation that the cells will eventually degrade and become useless over time.

Telstar could only be used when it was above the horizon so that radio waves could travel in a straight line from the satellite to a receiver. The satellite took ninety minutes to go around Earth. When it was out of position, below the horizon, it was out of operation. This did not discourage President John F. Kennedy who gave a speech suggesting that "All nations participate in a communication satellite system in the interest of world peace and closer brotherhood among people throughout the world."

A Cooperative Venture

The answer to the president's call was the International Telecommunications Satellite Organization (INTELSAT). The system is owned by member nations, each paying its share in relation to its amount of use.

Early Bird, a small cylinder weighing only eighty-six pounds (thirty-nine kilograms), went into orbit on June 28, 1965. Solar cells wrapped around it generated only forty watts of power. By today's standards, it was little more than a toy, but in 1965, it was considered revolutionary — the very first geostationary communication satellite. Designed to spin like a top, with an expected service of only eighteen months, *Early Bird* remained operational for four years.

Larger, but surprisingly cheaper to operate, *Intelsat 2* was launched in 1967. It became the first commercial satellite to be positioned over the Pacific Ocean.

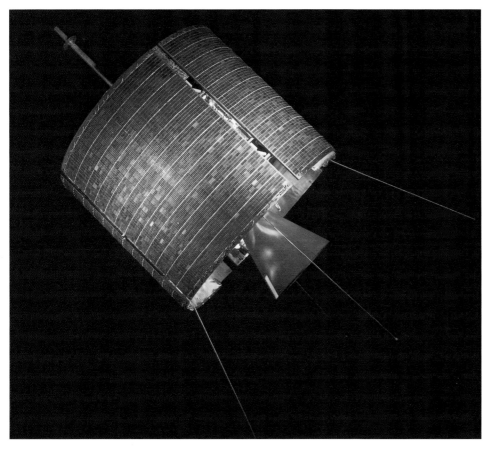

Early Bird, *sent into orbit in 1965, was the first geostationary communication satellite. As it spun around, thousands of solar cells on its surface absorbed energy from the Sun, generating the power to keep the satellite working.*

Keeping the World in Touch

The world's largest domestic satellite network was developed by the Soviet Union to help it reach all the remote corners of that vast nation. It helped to bring peoples with different cultures, customs, even languages, into closer contact with Moscow, the capital of the USSR. Starting in April 1965, the Soviets launched a series of satellites in highly elliptical orbits, reaching their highest point when over the northern hemisphere.

Other countries paid the United States to launch rockets to send up satellites for their own use. Canada launched *ANIK* on an American rocket in 1972. Other countries who subscribed to early satellite use were Australia, Brazil, India, China, and several Arab states. Indonesia found satellites especially useful in linking its scattered island nation.

Mae Jemison

"Don't be limited by others' limited imagination," says Dr. Mae Jemison, and she has followed that advice all her life. Born October

17, 1956 in Decatur, Alabama, at a time when women, especially women of color, were not expected to travel in space, she ignored the stereotypes of the day. As she read every book on astronomy she could find, she planned on becoming a scientist and eventually an astronaut.

Jemison has said that she owes her success in part to her teachers who, "let (her) go off and do things, explore on (her) own." She also credits her family for giving her confidence in her ability. Although born in Alabama, she considers Chicago, Illinois, her hometown. She attended Morgan Park High School, where she continued her interest in science, as well as other fields as varied as dance, art, and anthropology. An excellent student and a popular member of the pompom squad, she graduated at age sixteen and entered Stanford University in California with plans to major in chemical engineering and Afro-American studies.

One of the points she now stresses when talking to students around the country is to not limit their interests; a scientist should know what is going on in the world. "That means you have to find out about social science, art, and politics."

After receiving her B.S. degree in 1977, she enrolled in Cornell University Medical College in New York. Through her involvement with the American Medical Student Association, she traveled and studied in Cuba, Kenya, and Thailand. "It is interesting to see different ways of living," she has said.

Six months after being licensed as a medical doctor, she joined the Peace Corps, working in the West African country of Sierra Leone. At age twenty-six, she was one of the youngest doctors practicing in the area.

Still, she hadn't given up her dream to head for the stars. When NASA opened its selection process in October 1986, she applied — one of over two thousand applicants. When she received word that she had passed the first screening process, she recalls she couldn't stop smiling. When the final choices were made by NASA, she was one of only fourteen applicants selected, the first African-American woman to join the elite corps.

Five years of mental, emotional, and scholarly preparation preceded her first trip in space. On September 12, 1992, she was aboard the space shuttle *Endeavour*, conducting experiments dealing with weightlessness, tissue growth, and the development of semiconductor electrical material. The mission was arranged jointly by the U.S. and Japan. In yet another experiment, she worked with the fertilization and development of frogs in space. Back on Earth, the space-born tadpoles seemed to grow up as perfectly normal frogs. None of these experiments could have taken place without satellites to test life beyond our field of gravity.

Jan Davis and Mae Jemison at work on the Endeavour *shuttle mission in September 1992.*

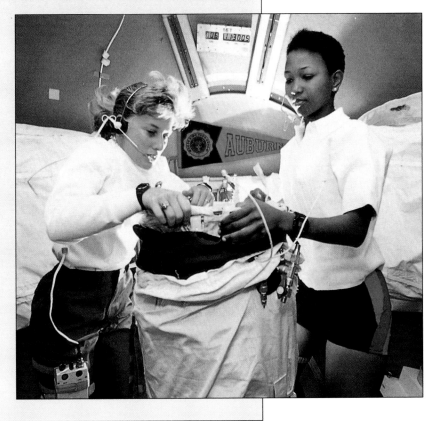

After resigning from NASA in March 1993, Jemison established a company that researches, develops, and markets advanced, space-based telecommunication systems to facilitate health care delivery in countries of the developing world. "We need to get every group of people in the world involved in space research because it is something that eventually we in the world community will have to share."

Receiving Stations and TV Satellites

At one time, the television networks used telephone lines and towers exclusively to transmit their signals. In some places, cables connected remote locations where TV signals were weak. But the growth of TV satellites was tremendous, from two stations in 1975 to thirty-four hundred in 1980. Almost twenty

An artist's impression of an Intelsat 7 communication satellite. The Intelsat 7 series was launched into geostationary orbits over the Pacific Ocean in the early 1990s. Each can carry up to ninety thousand voice channels and three TV channels simultaneously.

years later, that number has multiplied unbelievably. Today, many Earth stations receive the signals and feed them into cables serving individual homes. As a result, some predict that cable will one day be outmoded. Small dish antennae only one foot (thirty centimeters) across and costing only a hundred dollars or so are now available and do the job of directly feeding signals into home television sets.

Today, the entire world is connected by satellites in geostationary orbit. Whether ground stations are directing messages to the space shuttle or to your cordless phone, space science has changed the world's communication systems.

— Chapter 4 —
Predicting Weather

Benjamin Franklin was the first American to suggest that weather could be predicted. From newspaper articles, Franklin deduced that severe storms generally moved across the country from west to east. He further suggested that, if this were so, observers could follow a storm and notify those ahead of its path that it was coming. In some cases, they would have to be riding a pretty fast horse.

Franklin's ideas were finally put to practical use with the invention of the telegraph in 1837. Operators began to click their observations along telegraph wires to a central office where a national weather map was created.

Before the age of satellites, meteorologists still did not have enough specific information from around the world to put together the larger pieces of the weather puzzle. Information from extensive areas of our globe was unavailable, particularly from desert areas, polar ice caps, and ocean regions in both northern and southern hemispheres. Ground stations alone are unable to map upper air troughs and ridges and jet streams, where wind patterns develop in the upper atmosphere. Current information gained from satellites now fills these voids and reveals large-scale features of cloud movements and weather patterns.

Today, the World Weather Watch, a group of 147 countries cooperating to pool information, generates over forty thousand observations daily. Instruments are carried on ships, aircraft, buoys, balloons, and sounding rockets. Some of these isolated points of reference relay their information to satellites overhead that can immediately rebroadcast them to the United States

Weather Bureau. Speed is important to document the data, as our weather has a way of changing on a moment's notice.

Satellites Map Weather Patterns

Weather satellites come in many forms and have been launched by the United States, the Soviet Union, the European Space Agency, and Japan. In 1960, NASA placed in orbit the first TIROS (Television Infrared Observational Satellite). With its tiny TV cameras, TIROS flew over more than two-thirds of Earth's surface. Ten more weather satellites of this class were later deployed, and between 1964 and 1978, seven Nimbus satellites also were launched into space.

Low-flying weather satellites are placed in polar orbits. As they circle Earth, they take a picture of a strip of atmosphere below them a few hundred kilometers wide running from pole to pole. By itself, one strip doesn't give the whole picture, but with each pass, another strip of the world is recorded. At the end of each day, all these strips are put together, revealing the cloud cover over the entire Earth.

With just three satellites equally spaced high over the equator, the entire Earth can be seen at one time. Pictures can even be taken at night by looking at infrared radiation produced by heat stored in the clouds. Views from high-altitude satellites are shown by weather reporters as time-lapse sequences of cloud movements. Knowing just how fast weather fronts are moving can make predictions quite accurate.

In August 1979, meteorologists of the United States Weather

An artist's impression of the Nimbus-7 *satellite in orbit above Antarctica. One of its instruments, the Total Ozone Mapping Spectrometer, produced data that confirmed the existence of an ozone hole over Antarctica. Ozone in the upper atmosphere protects us from the Sun's harmful ultraviolet rays. By 1992, this ozone hole was almost as large as the North American continent.*

Data from a weather satellite was used by a computer to create this view of Hurricane Andrew, seen on the left as a thick swirl of cloud with a central eye, over the Gulf of Mexico. This hurricane caused devastation in Florida and Louisiana in 1992.

Bureau detected swirling clouds with an ominous black vortex racing across the ocean and the Gulf of Mexico, ready to hit land along a densely populated area. Ground stations had not predicted such a fierce storm, but warnings were issued and inhabitants evacuated before the worst of Hurricane David arrived. Whatever money had been invested in orbiting weather satellites proved well spent that day.

Wind from the Sun

Thanks to satellites, we are also learning about strange happenings in outer space. It wasn't a rainstorm that knocked out the power of Quebec, Canada, and disrupted service in seven states in northeast United States in 1989. It was the Sun.

In addition to light and heat, the Sun radiates an electrically charged gas, or solar wind. This energy is streaming out from the Sun toward Earth at an estimated million miles per hour. The hot, ionized gas, called *plasma*, carries magnetized particles outward, past the planets. Earth is shielded from the full blast of these particles by its own magnetic field.

Franklin Chang-Diaz

Dr. Franklin Chang-Diaz has traveled in space some eleven million miles aboard satellite space shuttles. He'll break that record in 1996 with another thirteen-day fling on the shuttle *Columbia*. He's

also traveled a few odd miles down on Earth — from his hometown, San Jose, Costa Rica, to astronaut headquarters in Houston, Texas. Along the way, he has accomplished some remarkable scientific research on some "far-out" subjects related to space technology and has received dozens of awards and honorary degrees.

Chang-Diaz was born on April 5, 1950, and graduated from Colegio de La Salle in San Jose in 1967. He later continued his education at the University of Connecticut, where he received a bachelor of science degree in mechanical engineering. His doctorate was earned at the Massachusetts Institute of Technology in 1977.

His early work was in the field of fusion reactors when he joined the technical staff of the Charles Stark Draper Laboratory. But in May 1980, Dr. Chang-Diaz was selected by NASA to become an astronaut, the first Hispanic to join the corps of space scientists. His talents were at once put to use in designing computer software programs for the space station to be built at the end of the century.

His first flight in space took place in January 1986, during which he participated in the deployment of the SATCOM KU satellite. On his next trip, in 1989, the crew aboard space shuttle *Atlantis* successfully deployed the *Galileo* spacecraft on its journey to explore Jupiter. Dr. Chang-Diaz also operated a sensitive ultraviolet instrument to map atmospheric ozone layers.

On his third trip, the European Retrievable Carrier Satellite (Eureca) was launched. In 1994, he was one of the crew on the first joint U.S. and Russian mission. These scientist-astronauts conducted a variety of biological experiments and collected data while observing weather patterns on Earth.

Dr. Chang-Diaz is an honored citizen of the United States, but he has not been forgotten in his homeland. In April 1995, he received the highest award ever given to a foreign citizen by the government of Costa Rica.

He is married to the former Peggy Doncaster of Louisiana, and the couple has two daughters. He enjoys music, glider planes, soccer, scuba-diving, hunting, and hiking, but his chief interests have always been looking toward the future. In fact, Chang-Diaz has already designed a new concept in rocket propulsion that will more economically and efficiently send satellites into orbit.

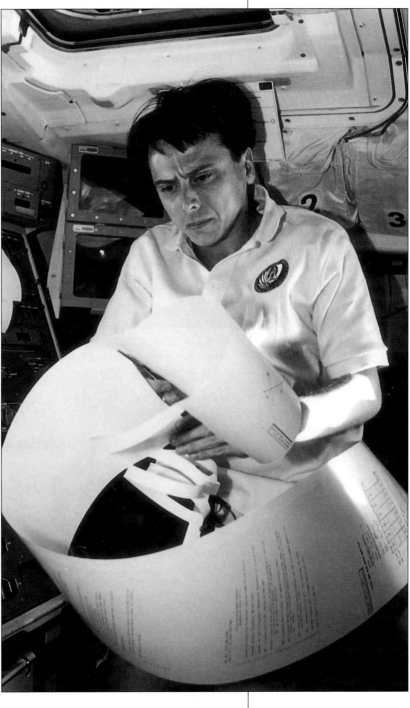

Franklin Chang-Diaz wrestles with one of the longest teleprinted messages in shuttle history aboard Discovery *in 1994.*

When the solar wind comes in contact with Earth's magnetic field, it creates a wild symphony of color we call the northern lights, or *aurora borealis*, in the Northern Hemisphere and the southern lights, or *aurora australis*, in the Southern Hemisphere. The existence of the solar wind was first confirmed in the early 1960s by NASA's *Mariner 2* spacecraft.

To help predict the potentially dangerous conditions that can disrupt our power sources, NASA launched the *Wind* satellite on November 1, 1994. It will study the mass, momentum, and energy of solar wind for the next three years. *Wind* was positioned in a circular orbit between the Sun and Earth to intercept the solar wind before it meets our own magnetic field. It will answer questions about the complex system of interacting plasma, magnetic fields, and electric currents, which can cause havoc by disrupting radio communication, navigational systems, and, as it did in March 1989, an entire nationwide electrical system.

Wind and Water

Climate changes usually follow a predictable pattern. Even in the tropics, where the weather is warm year-round, rainy seasons alternate with dry seasons, and each has its own distinct pattern of prevailing winds. However, the rhythm does change occasionally, and scientists are trying to discover the cause.

The name *El Niño* has been given to a change in the direction of ocean currents that recurs every five to ten years, resulting in exceptionally warm surface water along the coast of South America. The belt of warm water and the weather it brings stretches 5,000 miles (8,000 kilometers) across the equatorial Pacific. During normal years, the easterly (east to west) winds tend to drag the surface of the ocean along with them. The surface waters are deflected away from the equator in both directions, letting the colder, nutrient-rich water, well up from below. Tiny plants, on which fish feed, flourish on these nutrients. The surface waters become less productive if there is no upwelling of

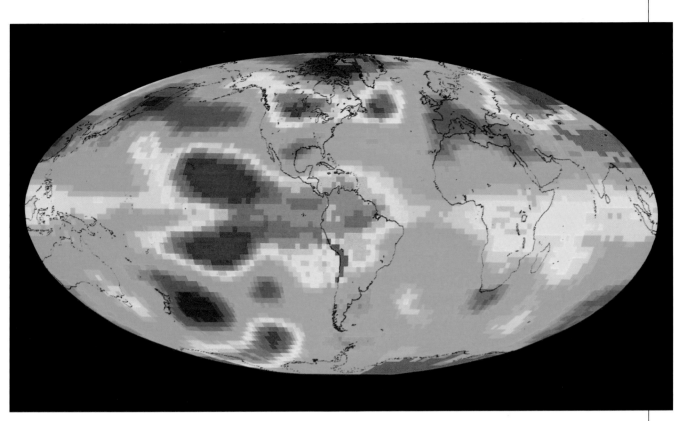

the colder water. When easterlies are blowing at full strength, the cold water along the equator also chills the air above it, making it too dense to rise high enough for water vapor to condense to form rain. Satellites equipped with infrared cameras can measure the water temperature and follow the path of the currents.

The 1982-83 El Niño was the strongest produced this century. It started in May 1982, when the strong easterly surface winds began to weaken and turned to westerlies accompanied by stormy weather. Soon, the ocean began to react to the changes. Sea levels rose along the shore of Ecuador, while in the western Pacific, the sea levels dropped to expose and destroy the upper layers of coral reefs. Warm water limited most fishing along the South American coast. When the fish disappeared, sea birds and seals died off. Heavy rainfall drenched the Peruvian coast.

Shifts in tropical rainfall affect wind patterns over much of the globe. Putting all this information together — wind speeds, ocean currents, layers of temperature differences — has helped

This false-color image of Earth, generated from TIROS satellite data, shows the temperature changes caused by the 1982–83 El Niño. Red areas are where the temperature is higher than normal, while blue areas indicate regions that are colder than normal. The large red area off the west coast of South America is where El Niño warms the surface waters of the Pacific.

meteorologists predict long-range pattern changes. For instance, floods can often be predicted, so knowing what to prepare for means less economic loss for farmers.

Fire and Ash

When Mount Saint Helens in Washington erupted on May 18, 1980, weather satellites looked on, warning aircraft pilots of the danger, as tons of volcanic ash were spewed into the atmosphere. Satellites have also saved lives and property from fire. Blazes can be detected by their smoke plumes, and the heat registered on infrared sensors. Thus wilderness fires in remote regions have been located and contained by prompt warning.

Ben Franklin may have started predicting weather patterns but he would not have believed how far we have come to understand weather. Unfortunately, we still have little control over it.

A crew member of the space shuttle Endeavour *took this photo of the plume from a newly erupted volcano on the Kamchatka Peninsula in far eastern Russia in October 1994. The area is part of a chain of volcanoes stretching south to Japan.*

Chapter 5
Earth Watch and Spies in the Sky

There's more to see than cloud patterns from a satellite focused on Earth. Observation satellites are used to map and monitor our planet's resources. In 1972, this new breed of satellite was named *Landsat*, meaning Land Survey Satellite; since then, four very successful satellites have taken pictures of virtually every bit of land surface on Earth.

Landsats evolved from the earlier weather satellites TIROS and Nimbus. They follow sun-synchronous, polar orbits. As a Landsat travels south, it passes on the sunlit side of Earth. It returns north on the dark side.

Dots of Color

No ordinary camera would do for Landsat pictures. Instead, scanning devices and television systems that produce strange colors are used. Trees show up as red, water is black, and cities appear blue. To scientists, every color has a very important meaning. Geologists, city planners, environmentalists, and agricultural researchers all use this valuable tool. Mapmakers can make up-to-the-minute changes on courses of river beds in time of flood.

One of the systems used is called the *multispectral scanner* (MSS). The MSS takes pictures the way you would read a book. Start in the upper left of the page, scan your eyes to the right, then drop down a line and repeat the process. Eventually, you have been able to see the whole page by scanning.

AMAZING FACTS

Residents of warm southern California are moving closer to Alaska whether they like it or not. Scientists estimate that southern California and Alaska will collide in approximately 150 million years. Satellites are keeping track of the movement.

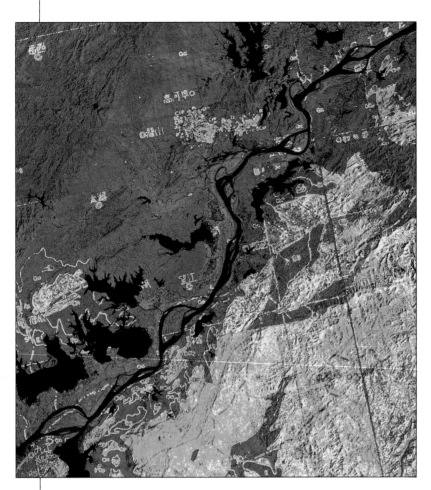

A false-color Landsat image indicates complex geological features in China's Anhui province. The dark diagonal line is the Yangtze River, and the large black areas are lakes. This sort of image helps scientists in mineral and oil prospecting.

As Landsat moves south, light from Earth passes through a prism that breaks it up into the colors of the rainbow. Each color identifies a chemical element. Other detectors are then aimed at these colors to measure the brightness of the light, and each color is converted into a number on a computer.

Each point on the computer scan is called a *pixel*, meaning picture element, and each pixel represents a spot on Earth, which is thirty-three yards (thirty meters) across. The MSS "sees" Earth in the green and red spectrum of visible light as well as in two regions of the infrared spectrum. On Earth, computers take the numbers and arrange them in their correct order to make the final pictures. It is possible to detect rivers, roads, large buildings, and rock formations. The MSS can even distinguish such features as different types of soil and vegetation.

Below and Above the Surface

With these pictures, geologists are sometimes even able to visualize what is below the surface of the land. They can see mountains and valleys and how the different types of rock lie against each other. Perfectly straight lines may indicate the place where an ancient earthquake splintered Earth's surface and wedged one layer of rock against another. The colors of the rocks and of the soil that lies on top can tell what minerals might be present.

Scientists know, for instance, what kind of rock will contain copper, tin, or iron, and they know what types of formations are good prospects for finding oil. The Heat Capacity Mapping Mission (HCMM), launched in 1977, was used to test what information could be discovered from the measurements of the Earth's temperature from space.

Landsat images are also used to locate sources of sea life and even fresh water. Hydrologists, scientists who study the world's water supply, are interested in knowing the extent of winter mountain snow cover. For many parts of the world, winter mountain snow is the main source for drinking water and irrigation water in the valleys below. Knowing the coverage helps hydrologists decide whether water rationing will be necessary during the next summer.

Even seafood supplies can be studied by looking for phytoplankton, microscopic floating plants coloring large areas of the oceans. Nothing seems too small for an eye in the sky to detect.

Rock formations and land use can clearly be seen in this Landsat image of the Bighorn Basin in Wyoming. The dark blue areas are irrigated fields along the Shoshone River, left and center, and Dry Creek, bottom right.

Many forms of pollution are also visible from space. Where factories are polluting nearby rivers and lakes, the water will appear discolored, and haze may hang over the region.

Crop Production and Urban Sprawl

Individual agricultural crops can also be defined from outer space. Satellites have been used to look at the progress of crops and to study vegetation growth. By measuring the greenness of plant chlorophyll, scientists can determine not only the health of crops but can pinpoint areas of drought. Researchers are trying to map out crop production for entire countries to foresee crop shortages.

Satellites have recorded the exact extent of the destruction of rainforest. Remarkable pictures of the encroaching Sahara desert

A Landsat photo of the junction of the Amazon and Negro Rivers. The Amazon appears blue because it carries a lot of sediment. Even after the rivers meet the waters do not mix at first. The large white area at the north of the junction is the city of Manaus. Most of the picture is Amazonian rainforest, broken by rivers (blue) and roads cut through the vegetation (white).

over once-agricultural areas have sent warnings to this part of the world that some solution must be found or people will be faced with the prospect of starvation.

Within urban areas, satellites show that cities are often sprawling out of control. Zoning laws have been written after studying pictures from space. Each snapshot is only of a moment in time, but taken together and added one to the other, these seemingly isolated, insignificant snapshots grow into a vast mosaic that is vital to the lives of everyone. They tell us something of the past and help us plan the future.

Secrets from the Past

Since satellites make it possible to study hundreds of square miles in a very short time, archaeologists have used pictures from outer space to determine where to dig for ancient cities that sometimes leave their outline in the soil that has covered them for centuries. One scientist is trying to find traces of Noah's ark as described in the Bible. Scientists have been successful in finding remnants of China's Great Wall that extend even further than the amazing 1,500 miles (2,400 kilometers) that we already know about.

Earth Wobbles

LAGEOS is a round satellite made of aluminum with a brass core. It is only 24 inches (61 centimeters) in diameter and yet weighs approximately 900 pounds (400 kilograms). This compact, dense design was selected to make the satellite's orbit as stable as possible as it looks at Earth.

Because Earth is not perfectly round nor equally dense through its interior, gravity varies from place to place around the globe. In addition, tides produced by the gravity of the Sun and Moon cause Earth's mass to shift in a space of hours. Studying these changes helps scientists understand the properties, as well as strength and behavior, of materials deep inside our Earth.

LAGEOS-2 undergoes prelaunch optical checks on its 426 equally spaced reflectors. This satellite monitors the area around the Mediterranean Sea, where movements of Earth's crust can be quite violent. The satellite is tracked from ground stations by laser beams that measure its position very precisely.

Earth's imperfect shape causes a small wobble in its rotation, much like the motion of a toy top. Satellites like LAGEOS have been able to detect changes in polar motion to an accuracy of two inches (five centimeters) and changes in the length of day to within one ten-thousandth of a second.

Military Satellites

The United States government has military forces stationed in many different parts of the world. All of them are kept in direct contact with each other, the Pentagon, and the White House by four satellites used expressly by the military.

The job of military satellites is two-fold: to coordinate all communication between task forces and to warn of attack. These satellites are orbiting in 22,300-mile (35,900-kilometer) high orbits. Should anything happen to them, replacements are waiting on standby to be launched into space.

Still others are 50,000 miles (80,000 kilometers) above Earth. These high-flying satellites are programmed as nuclear weapons detectors. Agreements have been signed by all major countries that no nuclear devices are to be detonated in the atmosphere. If any nation were to break the treaty, the world would immediately be warned of the danger. If it were discovered that satellites were armed with nuclear warheads, ways to defuse them from ground bases have been developed.

Low-orbiting satellites keep track of any unusual troop movements on the ground or at sea anyplace in the world. They can detect the building of airplane landing strips and missile installations. Satellite cameras are now so powerful it is said that it is possible to read numbers on a license plate from space.

If ever war is declared in the future, it is certain that satellites will be targeted for destruction. They are easy targets because they travel in specific orbits at specific speeds. An antisatellite weapon could be sensitive to heat waves, homing in for the kill. Powerful beams of laser light could also destroy the delicate instruments aboard a target satellite.

A lot of money and energy is being spent on defensive tactics it is hoped the world will never have to use. The more terrible the consequences of a future war, the more reluctant any nation will be to unleash its arsenal of destruction. Our use of satellites to protect and police outer space may be the surest path to peace.

A Defense Support Program (DSP) satellite about to be launched from the space shuttle Atlantis *in November 1991. DSP uses an infrared detector to sense heat plumes from missile launches and nuclear detonations.*

Edward Teller

No scientist in living memory has evoked such a swing of praise and criticism as Edward Teller. No one doubts his brilliance, but not all agree with his philosophy for peace.

Teller was born in Budapest, Hungary, in 1908 of well-educated, affluent parents. His childhood was thrown into chaos by political revolution with the communists trying to take over the government of Hungary, but this did not interrupt his schooling. He first attended the University of Budapest and later studied in southwestern Germany. His major field was chemistry, but he was drawn into the world of physics that Albert Einstein had suddenly opened up to questioning.

In 1930, twenty-two year old Edward Teller earned his Ph.D. in theoretical physics and was immediately offered a position in Denmark and later in London. His reputation was growing. He received proposals to come to the United States, being offered a full professorship at George Washington University in Washington,

Edward Teller speaks at a press briefing after an experimental underground atomic detonation in the New Mexico desert in 1961.

D.C. Recently married, he and his wife Mici set sail, destined to live in America for the rest of their lives.

In January 1939, startling news was announced that the atom had been split. Edward Teller was always the visionary, trying to see ten years ahead of his peers, getting a dozen ideas every minute, whether they were right or wrong. He sought to persuade the U.S. government to embark on a project to build the atomic bomb. It was the start of the Manhattan Project, work culminating in a blinding flash in the New Mexico desert with the world's first atomic explosion.

He next tried to design a "clean" bomb with no nuclear fallout that could be used for peaceful purposes. "If your mountain is not in the right place," he quipped, "just drop us a card."

Teller was one of the first scientists to warn that war might easily be waged in outer space. He urged the U.S. military to build up defenses against such a reign of terror launched by satellites. He had a plan to develop an x-ray laser beam that he predicted could clear the sky of enemy bomb-carrying satellites. The beam could be launched from the ground or from satellites put into orbit by the United States. Opponents of the idea feared that if an enemy satellite carrying nuclear ammunition were detonated in space, Earth's atmosphere would be contaminated. Teller next proposed to shower outer space with "smart rocks," later called "brilliant pebbles," to defuse enemy satellites by force of impact, not explosion.

In Teller's mind, satellites could be our salvation. His book, *Better a Shield than a Sword*, tried to waken the world to this new concept that satellites could be used as protection against war in outer space. This concept is gaining acceptance.

The most serious criticism his fellow scientists have is that he is overly enthusiastic without fully testing his ideas. But without a creative mind like Edward Teller's, the world would see little progress.

—— Chapter 6 ——
Finding the
Beginning of Time

On November 25, 1924, the *New York Times* newspaper carried an amazing article that quoted Dr. Edwin Hubble as saying that he had proof that some of the distant stars we see in the sky are "island universes" themselves, billions and billions of miles further into space than anyone had dreamed. These distant galaxies were so far away that light by which we are seeing them today left its source at the time dinosaurs roamed Earth.

The speed light travels is 186,000 miles (300,000 kilometers) per second. A light year is 6,000,000,000,000 (6 trillion) miles, the distance which light travels in one year. The distance Hubble was talking about was in millions of light-years.

The rest of Hubble's amazing theory was that the universe was expanding, flying apart, at tremendous speeds. Not everyone was ready to believe his theory, but as the power of Earth-bound telescopes increased and as astronomers were able to put telescopes on satellites above the cloudy layer of our atmosphere, his research has proven to be correct. Further study has placed these galaxies at even greater distances than Hubble had predicted.

Satellites Exploring the Universe

One of the most exciting uses of satellites is to stare at the cosmos to determine just what the universe was like shortly after the big bang, when a terrific explosion blew a concentrated core of matter into the void of space, the theory first introduced by Hubble himself. We are beginning to picture how our universe was formed and what its future may be by studying clouds of matter in the farthest reaches of space. We can watch these swirls of "dust" cluster together to begin new star systems. We are on the verge of understanding the mysteries of black holes in space, those swirling voids that suck matter into them, not allowing even light to escape.

On April 14, 1990, the 25,000-pound (11,000-kilogram) Hubble Space Telescope blasted into orbit amidst fiery flame and dazzling hopes. In spite of a faulty mirror, a mistake measured in fractions of a millimeter, the Hubble Space Telescope was seeing billions of miles farther than had ever been seen before, stretching

The Hubble Space Telescope separates from the Remote Manipulator System arm of space shuttle Discovery *in April 1990. The photo was taken from the shuttle's cabin by a crew member.*

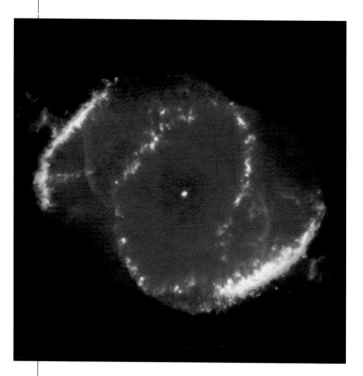

This image captured by the Hubble Space Telescope is of shells of gas (red and green) around a dying star (blue). It is made up of three exposures taken at different wavelengths. The complex patterns in the gas lead astronomers to believe that there is another unseen star orbiting the dying one.

the boundaries of our known map of space. Edwin Powell Hubble died in 1953, before satellites were a reality, but he had dreamed that some day an observatory could be placed on the Moon or on a space platform above Earth. He was honored by having such an instrument bear his name.

Space Telescopes

It has only been in the past decade that powerful telescopes like the Hubble and ultrafast supercomputers have been able to give astrophysicists the data they hunger for. They agree with the big bang theory. They also believe galaxies are strewn around the cosmos in patterns that have something to do with a mysterious dark matter that plays havoc with earlier notions of gravity between galaxies. Astrophysicists know about the nuclear reactions that power starlight and what chemicals the stars contain by seeing them in different energy wavelengths and through prisms and polarizing lenses, but they disagree on how old the universe must be.

Since Hubble's day, astronomers have agreed that you only need two pieces of information to deduce the age of the universe: how fast galaxies are flying apart and how far away they are. That doesn't leave a simple solution. It is very hard to tell how far away they are because they don't come in standard brightness, like a one hundred-watt light bulb.

Astronomy's most reliable light bulb is a type of star called a *cepheid variable*, whose brightness has been measured close to Earth. Cepheids couldn't be spotted more than a few galaxies away until the Hubble Space Telescope came into being. Astronomer Wendy Freedman and her team suddenly spotted their identifying "light bulb" cepheid in a faraway galaxy called M100. This has caused a furor that is not expected to quiet down until more satellites can be put in orbit to study the farthest reaches of space.

Freedman's measurements seem to place the age of our universe at about twelve billion years old, yet other experts claim that some of the oldest stars in our Milky Way galaxy are at least fourteen billion years old. "You can't be older than your Ma," quips Christopher Impey of the Steward Observatory in Arizona.

"Either we're close to a breakthrough, or we're at our wits' end," says astrophysicist Michael Turner. Satellites with ever more sophisticated equipment may some day soon give us answers. It is an exciting time to be looking at stars.

On the left is an image of spiral galaxy NGC 235 taken with a ground-based telescope. The color image on the right is of the center of this galaxy, taken with the Hubble Space Telescope's Wide Field Planetary Camera. The high resolution reveals gas patterns never seen before. There are also regions of intense star formation, including a bright super-compact star cluster.

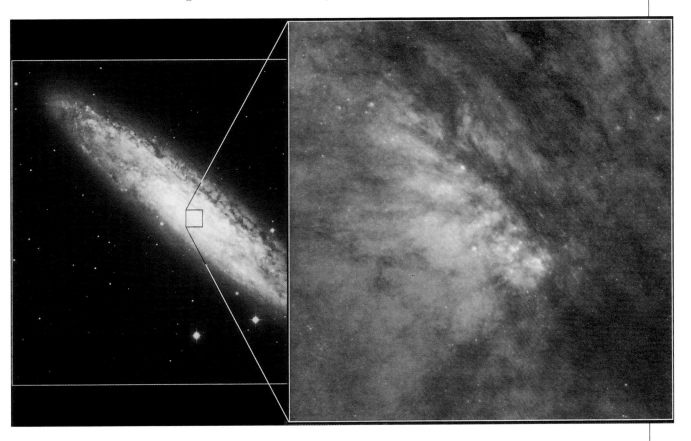

Other Wavelengths

Waves of energy, similar to the waves in the ocean, come in different heights, or amplitudes, measured from crest to trough.

They also come in different wavelengths, measured from one crest to another as they pass a given point. Before satellites were sent above our atmosphere, astronomers could only measure stars by the visible light energy we could see, although by the early 1930s, radio waves were detected in cosmic space. The advent of the space age and the satellites in the 1960s enabled astronomers to make observations at a whole new range of wavelengths. Progress was rapid, and much new data was obtained, particularly at ultraviolet, x-ray, and gamma-ray wavelengths.

Ultraviolet astronomy provides interesting information about the very low-density material found between distant galaxies. The distribution of this material is not even. In fact, big gas bubbles have been blown into it by very strong solar winds coming from the hot stars to be found in groups of recently formed stars.

Just as our Sun is losing matter from its atmosphere through the solar wind, the atmosphere of younger and more massive stars is blown away by similar solar winds. Data gathered by telescopes placed in orbit above our atmosphere are helping astronomers guess how these winds have shaped new stars, as well as scatter debris from older cosmic bodies like our Sun. Knowledge of these winds is very important in developing ideas of stellar evolution.

Observations in different wavelengths and through polarizing lenses have shown that some galaxies harbor in their midst nuclear objects that emit more energy than all the stars in the galaxy put together. What makes them so powerful? We hope to have answers soon.

Dr. Arthur Code aimed a special ultraviolet photo polarimetry telescope at clouds of matter. By viewing a dust cloud from different angles, using the light from different stars to illuminate the cloud, then measuring the polarized light reflected from the cloud, he was able to get a three-dimensional image more detailed than any before. This new view of our cosmos is helping astrophysicists write the history of the universe and predict what the future may be.

Chapter 7
Living in Space

The USSR was the first country to launch a piloted orbital space station in 1971, but on May 14, 1973, the United States followed with *Skylab*, the biggest orbital station ever built. It weighed one hundred tons (ninety-one metric tons), the largest artificial satellite ever put into orbit. The interior of its two-storey workshop measured more than 10,000 cubic feet (280 cubic meters) and boasted as many of the comforts of home as NASA engineers and scientists could provide.

The first compartment had two docking spaces, one for the Apollo spacecraft that would bring the astronauts to their working quarters and one for rescue craft. Seventeen feet (five meters) long and ten feet (three meters) in diameter, this room held controls for telescopes to study the Sun and stars and various instruments for studying Earth. It also contained a special furnace for experiments with welding, metal working, and crystal growing.

The far end of this compartment opened into an air lock module, a short tunnel with two doors, which cut off the tunnel

The Skylab *space station was operational during 1973, allowing three crews, each of three astronauts, to carry out experiments in space. Orbiting at an altitude of about 310 miles (495 kilometers),* Skylab *took more than 175,000 photos of the Sun and 46,000 of Earth.*

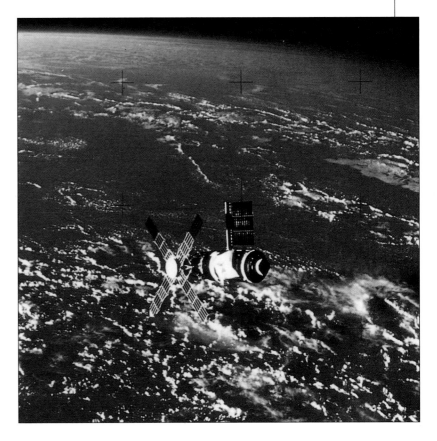

from the rest of the station. In the side of this air lock was a door leading to the outside of the station. Mission specialists used this door to enter and leave *Skylab* for walks in space. On such trips they would change the film in cameras mounted on the telescopes outside the cabin and carry on routine inspection tours to see that *Skylab* was surviving its long stay in space in good condition.

The door at the far end of the airlock led to the orbital workshop where the astronauts spent most of their time. This was forty-eight feet (fifteen meters) long and twenty-two feet (seven meters) in diameter, divided into two floors. A metal screening was all that paved the two levels, just enough to give the astronauts temporary footholds. The lower floor contained kitchen and sleeping quarters.

Some of the most important experiments were conducted on the astronauts themselves. How would their bodies adjust to zero gravity? Would their heart muscles grow sluggish, not able to keep them alive? Would their bones change texture? Doctors in space and on the ground monitored them constantly.

Three different crews were able to work here in space. Photos and data were analyzed and these helped later shuttle missions carry on further research. The mission of the *Skylab* was completed by the end of 1973, and scientists attempted to bring it back to Earth in 1979. *Skylab* burned up as it entered the atmosphere and crashed in a sparsely populated part of Australia.

The Soviet *Mir* space station has been orbiting Earth since February 20, 1986. The station

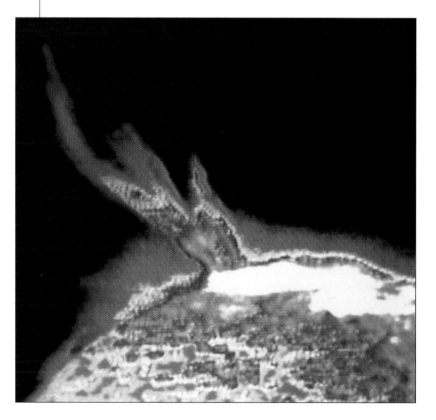

This ultraviolet image of a giant solar gas eruption was recorded from Skylab *in 1973. Clouds of gas are being catapulted into space by the Sun's distorted magnetic field.*

is locked alongside two independently operable units. Soviet cosmonauts have stayed in space for several months at a time, proving that men and women are able to adapt moderately well to zero gravity.

Space station Mir *taken from the shuttle* Discovery *during a rendezvous mission in February 1995.*

Space Experiments

Many experiments can be conducted on a space station or during shuttle flights that would not be possible on Earth. If you mix dirt and water on Earth, the heavier parts of the mixture will settle at the bottom of the jar. Not so in space. There is no gravity to pull the particles to the bottom. In space, mixtures stay mixed; this means it is possible to grow perfect crystals.

On Earth, if you put salt and water together, crystals begin to form, but their shapes vary greatly. If you do the same thing in a space lab, each crystal will be exactly the same. Certain kinds of crystals, such as quartz, are used in computers and other devices. Performance is much more reliable when the crystals are perfect.

Astronauts Norman Thagard and Stephen Oswald conduct a crystal growth experiment in the first International Microgravity Laboratory (IML-1). This was carried into orbit by space shuttle Discovery in 1992.

Earth-made microchips for computers must be processed in large vacuum tanks. Oxygen in the air causes chips to burn if they are heated to high temperatures, while nitrogen and other substances make chips change shape. Vacuums on Earth can remove most of the air, but never all of it.

Plus, producing certain pharmaceuticals would be much simpler in zero gravity. Crystals of protein grown in space are already used as research tools in developing drugs to combat cancer and other disorders.

Biological experiments have also been carried on in zero gravity. Seeing how fish adjust to zero gravity with no up or down to guide them may seem strange, but each experiment has its purpose in the larger picture of exploration. The second generation of fish tested seemed to get along just fine, though their parents had difficulties. Will this happen to humans who may someday not only explore space but live there?

Space Station *Freedom*

The United States has been planning a space station since the *Apollo 11* astronauts landed on the Moon, and, hopefully, one will be in place before the turn of the century.

Space station *Freedom* is our stepping stone to the solar system. A permanent orbiting research lab, it will be a proving ground for the hardware and procedures that will later be adapted for living and working on the Moon and Mars, including medical care facilities, improved space suits, materials and power systems, robots and automation, techniques for spacecraft assembly, and refueling in orbit.

Future satellites will be built in sections that can be assembled in different ways to meet different needs. They will be designed to be serviced and refueled in orbit so they can remain in space for years. When repairs are necessary, it will not always be necessary to call on space-suited astronauts. Instead, a robot repair satellite may be dispatched to do the job.

AMAZING FACTS

Private industry, as well as government-sponsored research, has had a great influence on expansion of space technology. AT&T Bell Laboratories claim some significant firsts. It is the birthplace of the transistor, laser, solar cell, light-emitting diode, electrical digital computer, cellular mobile radio, long-distance TV transmission as well as many major contributions to the telecommunication network. It has received more than twenty-five thousand patents, averaging one per day since its founding in 1925.

Bruce McCandless II

On February 7, 1984, Captain Bruce McCandless became the first human satellite to ever orbit Earth without a tether connecting him to the space shuttle. Actually he was traveling at 17,000 miles per hour (27,000 kilometers per hour), the same speed as the orbiting shuttle. Yet there was no sensation of speed, only a feeling that he was floating on a sea of space. There was no atmosphere to cause wind or friction as he somersaulted and twisted and turned 175 miles (282 kilometers) up in space.

Only a remarkable jet-powered backpack kept him from drifting off into space forever. There had been no way to give this equipment its final test on Earth. Only as a floating satellite could McCandless begin to activate his nitrogen-powered rockets to propel him in any direction.

Twenty-four separate nozzles gave him the thrust. When an astronaut begins moving in a certain direction, he or she will keep moving in that direction indefinitely until an opposite thrust is applied, sort of like applying a brake. It is a tricky maneuver to apply just the correct amount of jet pressure so as not to spin out of control. It took plenty of courage to float alone in space, but McCandless had been working long hours in a laboratory overseeing the creation of this complicated piece of equipment; he had confidence that he could control it.

Bruce McCandless was born June 8, 1937, in Boston, Massachusetts. He received a bachelor of science degree from the U.S. Naval Academy in 1958. He went on to earn a masters of science degree in electrical engineering from Stanford and subsequently received flight training in Pensacola, Florida, and Kingsville, Texas. He had logged over fifty-two hundred hours flying time before he tackled his solo performance in outer space.

His fifteen million-dollar backpack looked like a seatless chair with arms that extended on either side where the controls were placed. On that memorable day when he stepped out of the shuttle cargo bay and headed away from the mother satellite ship, he cautiously slowed his pace. When he was about three football fields distance away, he experimented with twists and turns to evaluate just how useful the equipment would be when eventually used in the building of the future space station.

All went well, and he shouted into his intercom system with a verbal bow to Neil Armstrong's famous comment when landing on the moon, "That may have been one small step for Neil, but it was a heck of a long leap for me." He continued in a light vein. "Do you want me to do windows or anything else while I'm out here?"

When he was later asked by President Ronald Reagan how it felt to be alone in outer space, his answer was that the view was terrific, but more important, he had proved that astronauts could help build bigger and better satellites in outer space with such wonderful new sophisticated equipment.

Bruce McCandless floats freely above the shuttle's cargo bay, propelled by his jet-powered backpack, the Manned Maneuvering Unit (MMU).

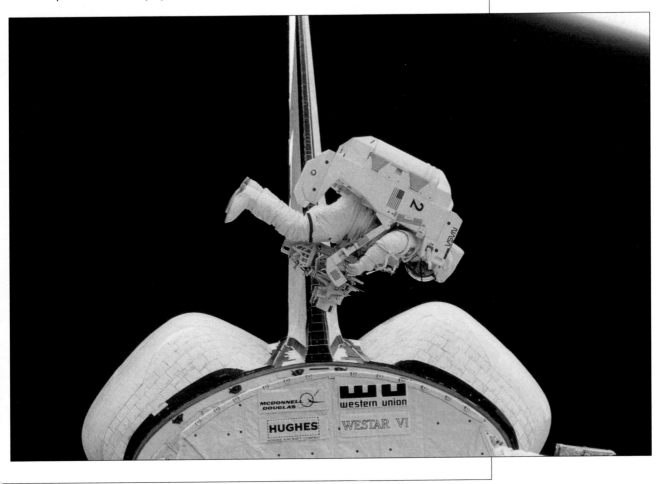

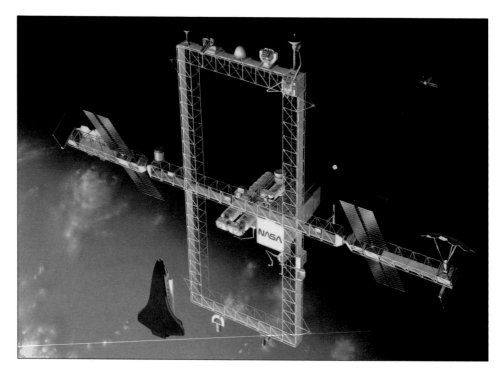

An artist's impression of space station Freedom *with a shuttle about to dock. The structure will be assembled in space and be permanently occupied. It will contain laboratory modules provided by the U.S., Japan, and the European Space Agency.*

Space station *Freedom* will be a good stopover on our future trips to the Moon. Many have asked why we want to go back to the Moon. First, because it is nearby, just three days from Earth. The back side of the Moon, rock stable and isolated from the electronic noise of Earth, is a perfect platform for the next generation of astronomical observatories. It may also be possible to mine oxygen from the lunar soil to refuel spacecraft or for life support. There we can learn to live on another world, with its reduced gravity and hostile environment.

Surprises in Space

Sometimes our greatest discoveries come when we least expect them. We may be looking at the stars to study the beginning of time, but by chance come upon a new method for manufacturing energy for use on Earth. Many items, such as Teflon and fireproof roofing material, have been developed with research in space. Material science may provide useful alloys, faster, more efficient electrical semiconductors, or ways to combat diseases here on Earth. One of the most ambitious plans is to create huge solar cells that may one day be able to capture solar energy and convert it to electricity for beaming to Earth.

Busy Signals

Our airwaves are getting more crowded with all the communication satellites we have been launching. We do not want to continually clutter the space above Earth with too much traffic, as interference will result. Many future satellites will be clustered together to save orbital space and cost. Platforms will have large solar cell panels to take care of satellite clusters.

A future communication satellite may be as large as an entire city block. In some designs, hundreds of small antennae will be mounted on a platform, each aimed in a different direction.

The Past, Present, and Future with Satellites

Satellites will continue to serve us on Earth by relaying our messages, by watching our atmosphere, by helping us locate and protect our resources, and by giving us clear glimpses of our universe.

The most compelling reason for studying what is out there in space was given by astronomer Arthur Code. "Studying these distant stars and the ejection of matter from stars is all part of the study of how our planet was formed and of how we came to be. . . . The stuff you are made of was at the center of some star. You are part of a star. That is your legacy."

Satellites are helping us not only to study space but also to discover who we actually are.

Space shuttle Atlantis *commander Robert Gibson greets* Mir *space station commander Vladimir Dezhurov after the docking of the two vehicles on June 29, 1995. This was the climax of a carefully planned exercise in international space cooperation. All the shuttle astronauts went aboard* Mir, *meeting the Russian crew and fellow astronaut Norman Thagard, who had been on* Mir *for several months.*

Timeline

1957 — First artificial satellite, *Sputnik*, is launched by the Soviet Union.

1958 — First U.S. satellite, *Explorer*, is launched.

1960 — First passive communications satellite, *Echo I*, is launched from Cape Canaveral, Florida. NASA deploys first Television Infrared Observational Satellite (TIROS) to observe the weather.

1961 — Yuri Gagarin circles Earth in the first space flight by a human.

1962 — First American orbital flight as John Glenn travels in space.

1965 — *Early Bird*, first geostationary communication satellite, is launched.

1969 — Neil Armstrong becomes the first man to walk on the surface of the Moon.

1972 — First Landsat Earth-mapping satellite is launched.

1973 — First crew occupies *Skylab*, the largest artificial satellite to date.

1981 — First orbital flight of the space shuttle *Columbia*.

1982 — Space shuttle *Columbia* launches a pair of commercial satellites.

1984 — Astronaut Bruce McCandless becomes the first human satellite as he tests the powered Manned Maneuvering Unit, moving independently in space without being tethered to the space shuttle.

1986 — Soviet *Mir* space station comes into operation.

1990 — Hubble Space Telescope is placed in orbit.

1994 — NASA launches *Wind* satellite to study solar wind.

1995 — AT&T receives authorization to launch three new high-power satellites for U.S. commercial service to revolutionize transmission quality and capacity to handle future increased demands on communication service.

Further Reading

Asimov, Isaac. *Rockets, Probes, and Satellites.* Milwaukee, WI: Gareth Stevens, 1988.

Baker, David. *Earth Watch.* Vero Beach, FL: Rourke, 1989.

Barrett, Norman. *The Picture World of Rockets and Satellites.* New York: Franklin Watts, 1990.

Bendick, Jeanne. *Artificial Satellites.* New York: Franklin Watts, 1982.

Branley, Franklyn Mansfield. *From Sputnik to Space Shuttles.* New York: Crowell, 1986.

Dudley, Mark. *An Eye to the Sky.* New York: Crestwood, 1992.

Fields, Alice. *Satellites.* New York: Franklin Watts, 1981.

Sabin, Francene. *Rockets and Satellites.* Minneapolis, MN: Troll, 1985

Van Horn, Larry. *Communications Satellites.* New York: Grove Enterprises, 1987.

Glossary

Astrophysicist: A scientist who studies the physics of stars, planets, other heavenly bodies, and the universe.

Atmospheric ozone: A gas that forms a thin layer in the upper atmosphere and protects life on Earth from untraviolet rays. Each molecule of ozone consists of three atoms of oxygen.

Black hole: An object in space whose gravity is so great that nothing, not even light, can escape from it and that sucks in matter from around it.

Cepheid variable: A type of star with measurable variations of energy, helping astronomers judge distance in outer space.

Elliptical orbit: A path shaped like a narrow or flattened circle that some satellites fly in.

Gamma rays, x-rays, infrared rays, microwave rays, and light rays: All forms of electromagnetic radiation with different frequencies that are studied in outer space as well as on Earth.

Geostationary orbit: The path of a satellite whose rotation has been made to synchronize with the rotation of Earth, making it appear to remain stationary over a given point on Earth.

Laser beam: Energy that is concentrated in a powerful, narrow beam of light with identical wavelengths and frequencies. Lasers can cut through materials as hard as diamonds or as delicate as the human eye.

Pixel: Single dot on a computer screen.

Plasma: Hot ionized gas radiating from the Sun.

Polarized light: Light that has waves that vibrate in only one direction.

Solar cells: Devices that convert sunlight into electrical energy.

Sun-synchronized polar orbit: A satellite's path that circles Earth over its poles and is coordinated with Earth's movement around the Sun.

Telemetry encoders: Computers that track the onboard equipment of satellites and relay information to Earth.

Index

Numbers in *italic* indicate pictures; numbers in **bold** indicate biographies